Gregor Mendel

Gregor Mendel

GENETICS PIONEER

DELLA YANNUZZI

FRANKLIN WATTS
A Division of Scholastic Inc.
New York Toronto London Auckland Sydney
Mexico City New Delhi Hong Kong
Danbury, Connecticut

For my daughter Cara, a future physician

Photographs © 2004: AKG-Images, London: 30, 33, 54, 57, 60; American Philosophical Society Library, Philadelphia/Curt Stern Papers: 29, 43; Bridgeman Art Library International Ltd., London/New York: 34 (Archives Charmet), 28 (Ali Meyer), 25 (Roger-Viollet, Paris); Corbis Images: 2, 76, 92, 94 (Bettmann), 70 (Aaron Horowitz); Getty Images/Mario Tama: 95; Hulton | Archive/Getty Images: front cover, 71; Margaret H. Peaslee, Ph.D., Professor of Biology, University of Pittsburgh at Titusville: 8, 14, 56, 66, 73; Mary Evans Picture Library: 16 (Pictorial Times), 15, 63; Natural History Museum, London: back cover ghost; Peter Arnold Inc.: 22 (James L. Amos), 11 (A. Reidmiller); Photo Researchers, NY: 50 (Archive), 78 (Dr. Jeremy Burgess/SPL), 26, 97 (James King-Holmes/SPL), 46 (Laguna Design/SPL), 38 (Tom Mchugh), 32, 83 (SPL), 53 (Sheila Terry); Stepan Bartos: 68, 86; Visuals Unlimited: 39 (Wally Eberhart), 59 (Jana R. Jirak), 41 (R.W.Van Norman).

Library of Congress Cataloging-in-Publication Data

Yannuzzi, Della.
   Gregor Mendel : genetics pioneer / by Della Yannuzzi.
      p. cm. — (Great life stories)

Summary: Discusses the life and work of Gregor Mendel, an Austrian monk who studied heredity in plants and is considered the father of genetics.

Includes bibliographical references and index.
   ISBN 0-531-12263-8
   1. Mendel, Gregor, 1822–1884—Juvenile literature. 2. Geneticists—Austria—Biography—Juvenile literature.
[1. Mendel, Gregor, 1822–1884. 2. Geneticists. 3. Scientists.]   I. Title. II. Series.

   QH31.M45Y36 2004
   576.5'2'092—dc22

                                                                            2003016960

1 2 3 4 5 6 7 8 9 10 R 13 12 11 10 09 08 07 06 05 04

Contents

ONE

A Farmer's Son

Johann Mendel was born on July 22, 1822, the second child and only son of Anton and Rosine Mendel. His older sister Veronika had been born in 1820, and a younger one, Theresia, would follow in 1829. Two other children were born into the family but died soon after birth. Mendel and his family lived in a small village called Heinzendorf, now called Hyncice, in a region named Northern Moravia. Moravia is now part of the Czech Republic.

The Mendel family farmed land owned by the Countess Maria Truchsess-Ziel. The Mendels had an arrangement with the countess that required the family to work the land and give the countess part of their crops in exchange for the right to farm and live on the land.

This is the house where Johann (later called Gregor) Mendel grew up.

This arrangement was part of what is called the feudal system, in which people were allowed to live on and farm land that belonged to a noble person or landowner. The farmers were required to share some of their crops with the landowner and kept the rest to sell or use. Sometimes, there was a mill on the property used to grind wheat. The farmer could use the mill, but he also had to grind the land-owner's wheat or pay to use the mill. Anton Mendel had to work three days a week on the countess's estate lands for the privilege of living on her land.

LEARNING ABOUT NATURE

Johann's father and mother worked hard to provide for their family. They lived in a brick house Anton Mendel had built on land the family had farmed for many years. The Mendel family also owned two horses. They were not poor, but money was scarce. Johann worked with his father in the fruit orchards and fields and helped take care of the beehives. He liked nature and was curious about how living things developed and grew. His interest in the natural world was encouraged by his environment. Moravia was an area where people earned their living through agriculture and the breeding of sheep. Farmers were always looking for better ways of improving their livestock or getting better fruit from their trees. They experimented through selective breeding, which is a method of choosing and breeding the best specimens of animals and crops. At this time, the farmers didn't know how traits were passed on from generation to generation. They just knew that selective breeding worked.

Johann's interest in nature and the world around him was influenced by both the natural environment, and his father. Anton Mendel taught his son how to replace old varieties of fruits with better ones through a method called grafting. The grafting of fruit trees has been used for hundreds of years. It is a way to create new plants, make better ones, repair damaged plants, and save trees that are in danger of becoming extinct. It is done by making a cut into a host plant (one that is in the ground) and taking a cutting from another plant. This second cutting is called the scion. It is set into the cut in the host plant. When the two grow together and form new tissue, it is call a graft.

The Czech Republic

Today, the area in which Johann Mendel lived and worked is called the Czech Republic. In 1918, the Czechs and their neighbors, the Slovaks, formed a new republic called Czechoslovakia. In 1993, Czechoslovakia split into two separate countries, the Czech Republic and Slovakia. The Czech Republic is a small country in the center of Europe, divided into three provinces: Bohemia to the west, Moravia to the east, and Silesia, which is situated along the border with Poland.

Johann's father taught him a lot about the natural world and how to care for plants.

Anton Mendel expected his son to take over the farm one day. If Johann didn't do this, the farm would have to be sold. Johann, however, wanted to get an education.

GETTING AN EDUCATION

The family farm required many long hours of labor. Johann's mother Rosine knew how difficult it was to work the land. Her family had

Early Thoughts on Heredity

During Mendel's youth, most people thought that parents and their children resembled each other because of a blending of traits inherited from each parent. For example, if one parent had brown hair and the other parent had blond hair, a child born to them may have dirty blond hair. Others thought there was something in the blood that was responsible for passing on traits such as hair or eye color. The Greek philosopher and scientist Aristotle believed that each offspring was a combination of elements from both parents' bodies. He thought that the blood of both mixed together and traits were then passed on to future generations. When Antoni van Leeuwenhoek developed the microscope in the 1600s and life-forms were scientifically observed, theories on heredity began to change.

been in the gardening business for years. She wanted her son to get an education, so she encouraged him to study. Johann was able to attend the free village grammar school, but the family couldn't afford to pay for any further schooling. Fortunately, a schoolteacher named Thomas Makitta and the village priest, Father Schreiber, made it possible for Johann to continue his schooling. First, they had to convince Johann's father that his son should be allowed to develop his love for learning. Anton Mendel agreed, although he wanted his son to remain on the family farm.

Thomas Makitta and Father Schreiber arranged for Johann to attend a school in a nearby town run by the Piarist Fathers, a religious order. The fathers agreed not to charge any teaching fees, but the family would have to pay for Johann's room and board. At the age of eleven, Johann Mendel said good-bye to his family and traveled to the nearby town of Lipnik.

Johann did so well in his classes that he was always at the top of his class. The Piarist grammar school was a good one, but it wouldn't prepare him to go on to a university. He needed to go to a gymnasium—a type of school—in the town of Troppau (now named Opava). Once again, the problem of money arose and brought with it the stress of moving to another town. Anton and Rosine Mendel contributed some funds for Johann's room, food, and classroom materials, but Johann had to find part-time work to pay the rest of the costs. He was only twelve years old.

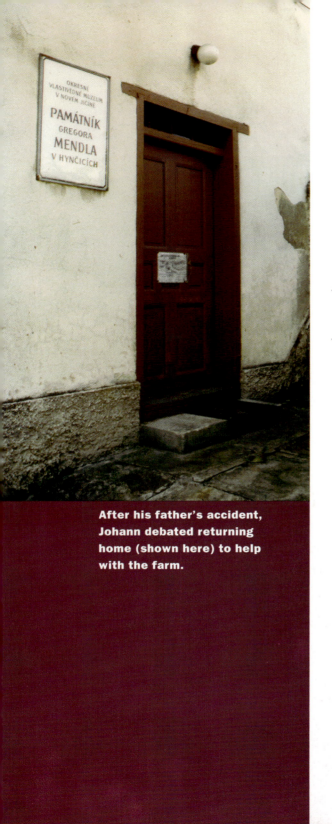

After his father's accident, Johann debated returning home (shown here) to help with the farm.

Johann met many different students at the gymnasium. The majority of them were not farmer's sons, but of a higher social position. Because of his background, Johann may have been ridiculed by some of his classmates. They may have made fun of Johann's worn clothes and lack of money. It was difficult for him, but Johann managed to tutor his fellow students for a fee and still earn high marks. He took a special interest in the natural sciences. By the age of sixteen, he had finished four of the required six years needed to graduate.

In 1838, Johann's family experienced misfortune. His father Anton was hit by a falling tree and was unable to perform the farmwork. The Mendels told their son they couldn't send him any more money. Johann didn't know what to do. He could not continue his studies without his family's financial support. The strain of studying, working, and worrying about how he could afford to continue his education was taking its toll on his mind and body. He had a difficult decision to make. He had choose whether he was going to continue his education or return to the family farm and become a farmer.

Johann worried about whether he would be able to continue his education. This engraving shows what an European school may have looked around the time Mendel attended school.

Many students with little money turned to tutoring as a way to earn enough to continue their educations.

A Life of Learning

Although he did not want to disappoint his family, Mendel chose to pursue his education. He decided to become a private tutor in order to pay his expenses while still attending school. He enrolled in the required teaching courses and took an exam to qualify him for tutoring.

ILL HEALTH

After a brief visit home to see his family, Mendel returned to his studies and to teaching. He enjoyed tutoring, although his days were often long and tiring. He had to divide his time between schoolwork and earning money to feed, clothe, and house himself. These long, work-filled days began to slow him down mentally and physically. His body couldn't tolerate such a demanding schedule. In the spring of 1839, Mendel became ill and was forced to return to the family farm. He spent long days in bed while his mother Rosine cared for him until he grew stronger. By the fall of 1839, Mendel was well enough to return to the school at Troppau. He was more determined than ever to graduate with his class. On August 7, 1840, Mendel earned his certificate with high honors. He was eighteen years old.

Mendel's desire to learn was strong even though his life was filled with many hardships. His goal was to attend a university, but he still had to complete another two years of schooling at a philosophical institute. The closest one was in the city of Olmutz, now renamed Olomouc. In the fall of 1840, he traveled to Olmutz and signed up for courses in philosophy, theology, math, and physics. He struggled through the first few difficult months. As always, he faced the problem of supporting himself financially. He did not know anyone in the city and had a hard time finding tutoring work. He was lonely, tired, and often hungry because he didn't have enough to eat. He kept in contact with his family, often writing letters to his mother about his fears and hopes. Finally, Mendel could no longer take the stress. His body and mind needed some rest. He stopped his studies and once again left for home and the security and comfort of his loving family. His mother and sister Theresia took care of him for nearly a year. Then Mendel had some good luck, thanks to the sale of the family farm and to his younger sister's generous offer.

BACK TO SCHOOL

Mendel's father sold his farm to Alois Sturm, the husband of Mendel's older sister Veronika. The terms of the contract stipulated that Johann receive money from the farm sale for his education. In addition, extra money would be paid to him if he should enter the priesthood. The contract also stated that a dowry be set aside for his sister Theresia, should she marry. Theresia decided to give her brother a part of her dowry ahead of time for his studies. Johann was so moved by his sister's offer that in later years, he gave money to his three nephews for their college studies.

His Sister's Dowry

Money from the sale of the Mendel family farm was set aside for Theresia's dowry. A dowry is the money, items, or land that changes hands between families that are to be joined through a marriage. In Theresia's case, if she were to marry, she and her family would give the dowry to her groom's family. In other cultures, sometimes the groom's family gives something to the family of the bride.

It was the fall of 1841, and Mendel was nineteen years old. He was still committed to his life of learning, which was made easier by his family's support and sacrifice. At least for the time being, he could continue at the institute without worrying whether he would eat every day. In time, he was even able to find students to tutor.

Mendel was also fortunate in another way. One of his teachers, Professor Friedrich Franz, saw promise in the young student whose favorite subjects were mathematics and physics. He recognized Mendel's talents and his interest in the natural sciences. Professor Franz was a physics teacher and an Augustinian monk. He became Mendel's friend and mentor. Mendel could not have hoped for a better teacher. Franz had been teaching physics for more than twenty years. He was a capable scientist who opened Mendel's eyes to the scientific world. Mendel's interest in exploring the world of science began in Franz's physics class. Franz knew about his student's struggle to get an education. He admired Mendel for his bright mind and determination to succeed.

In the summer of 1843, Mendel graduated with honors from the philosophical institute. He could now apply to a university and work toward his college degree. However, his money was running out again. For the past twelve years Mendel had been struggling to pay his way through school. He did not want to give up now, but attending the university would cost more money, and the studies would be more difficult. To cover his expenses, he would have to find tutoring work again. He was only twenty-one years old, but didn't know if he could handle another four years of struggling. Mendel worried about whether he would get sick again and have to return home. He was uncertain about his future. Unless some more good fortune came his way, he would have to end his dream of getting a college education.

It was not long before help was offered to Mendel. It meant he would have to make some changes in his life, but Mendel was thankful that, at last, the burden of relying on his family and tutoring would be removed.

Mendel's teacher thought he should join the Augustinian order. This order still continues to this very day.

THREE

New Directions

The answer to Mendel's call for help came from his physics teacher and mentor, Professor Franz, who taught at the philosophical institute as well as at the University of Vienna. Franz had been in contact with the abbot, or leader, of the Augustinian order at St. Thomas Monastery in Brünn. The Augustinians were a scholarly order, interested in research, science, and education. The Moravian Catholic Church agreed with scientists and educators that academics and science were important to encourage. When Emperor Francis Joseph authorized clerics to supervise the teaching of math and biblical studies at Brünn's philosophical institute, the monasteries needed bright men to become teachers. Professor Franz thought Mendel was a good candidate to join the Augustinian order.

Mendel listened carefully to Professor Franz's proposal. He valued and respected Franz as a teacher and a friend. Under his instruction, Mendel had developed his lifelong interest in physics and mathematics. Although Mendel had not planned to become a monk, his teacher's suggestion that he consider this vocation appealed to him. He could continue his education and be free from financial worries. The Augustinian order would take care of his financial needs. Mendel talked to his parents and received their consent. He then applied to the monastery and was one of thirteen candidates accepted as a novice, or a person given membership in a religious community, in October of 1843. On entering the Augustinian order, he chose another name, Gregor, which was the custom when entering a monastery.

MENDEL BECOMES A MONK

The St. Thomas Monastery was located in the oldest part of Brünn near the banks of the Schwarza River. In 1783, the Augustinian monks occupied a building previously inhabited by nuns. Above the monastery, on a cliff, stood a thirteenth-century fortress called Spilberk Castle.

Mendel was attracted to the Augustinian order because it was considered liberal within the Catholic Church. Unlike other orders, such as the Benedictines or Carthusians, who practiced certain rules of discipline, ate sparingly, and lived in isolation, the Augustinian order allowed open communication, intellectual freedom, and the opportunity to leave the monastery and go out into the community. Many of the monks were teachers, scientists, and philosophers who worked and taught at local schools. The Augustinian community was an interesting and challenging one. There were always plenty of activities, ideas, books, and community projects for the monks to explore. One of Mendel's favorite places was the monastery library, which contained twenty thousand books. It was a quiet, private place where he spent many enjoyable hours doing research or reading favorite books.

The monastery where Mendel lived was near Spilberk Castle, which can be seen in the background of this engraving.

With his love of learning, Mendel found the library with its extensive collection of books to be a haven.

The monastery was able to offer accommodations for forty-two monks. The safety and security this small community offered was exactly what Mendel needed in order to lead a healthy, productive, and comfortable life. As he once said, "It was difficult earning a living and I could no longer endure any more exertion. I felt compelled to free myself from the struggle to survive." Now, Mendel no longer had to worry about money or how he would finish his education.

Mendel was content with his new life. As a novice, he worked in the monastery's botanical garden, which satisfied his interests in science and nature. He had even started a friendship with an older monk named Matous Klacel who had many interesting views. Klacel taught philosophy, but he was also interested in natural science and wrote nature and science articles. Klacel was also in charge of the monastery's experimental garden. Mendel was drawn to Klacel's freethinking ideas and expertise in gardening.

The Augustinians

The philosophy of the Augustinian order is "knowledge to wisdom." The order offered Mendel a religious life as well as a learned one. The order's namesake was St. Augustine, a bishop and philosopher who lived in fourth century. St. Augustine wrote several important religious and philosophical works, including *Confessions* and *The City of God*. He is considered by many to be one of the most influential and significant thinkers of all time.

Austria's Emperor Francis Joseph

The man who ruled Mendel's world was a descendant of the Hapsburg royal family, which had been in power since the 1200s. The Hapsburgs' original land holdings in northwest Switzerland and Alsace (now a part of France) increased in size over the years through royal marriages between countries and lands won in wars. In 1815, Austria was the largest country in Europe, apart from Russia. When Emperor Francis Joseph was crowned ruler of Austria in 1848, he was only eighteen years old (shown here as a young child). His land holdings included most of Central Europe. Emperor Francis Joseph ruled over people from diverse ethnic groups. There were Czechs, Slovaks, Serbs, Ukrainians, Polish, Germans, Italians, and several other groups, but one-fifth of the population was German and the official language of the empire was German. In 1867, the Austrian Empire became the dual monarchy of Austria-Hungary. Emperor Francis Joseph ruled his large empire for nearly sixty-eight years, until his death in 1916 at the age of eighty-six.

In 1848, Klacel asked Mendel to take over the garden. Klacel had been assigned a new job as the monastery's librarian. Throughout the years, Klacel had upset the Catholic Church and the Hapsburg government with his political views supporting the abolishment of the feudal system and his support of a Czech national movement. Mendel and Klacel remained close friends until Klacel's death in 1882.

When Mendel was not in the garden or in the library, he spent most of his time studying languages and theology at the Brünn Theological College. After four years of study, he became an ordained priest on

This portrait of Mendel and his fellow monks was taken around the time that Mendel became an ordained priest. Mendel is in the back row, second from the left.

August 6, 1847. After he was ordained, Brother Mendel became an assistant pastor at a local church. He also did chaplain service, leading religious services and counseling sick people at a hospital. Continuing his interest in learning, he studied for a doctoral degree in philosophy. Mendel tried to enjoy his work, but he did not do well with ill or dying people because of his sensitive nature. He became ill again and could no longer handle his duties.

The City of Brünn

More than two hundred years ago, about twenty thousand people lived inside the old city walls of Brünn. It was a city full of religion, culture, and intellectual pursuits. There were many churches, schools, and science and agricultural organizations. In 1918, its Czech name became Brno. Brno is the second largest city in the Czech Republic and is the capital of the region of Moravia. Brno is a large, industrial city with a population of close to 400,000 people.

BECOMING A TEACHER

Mendel was fortunate in that the abbot of the monastery, Father Cyrill Franz Napp, was a sensitive, kind man. He was a scientist, teacher, thinker, and member of the Brünn Agricultural Society. He was interested in plants and gardening, and once mentioned to Mendel that the process of heredity could be explained through experimentation. He wanted his monks to be happy and to carry out their duties according to their interests and inner needs. He encouraged their educations and allowed them to pursue independent activities. Abbot Napp could see that working at a hospital and comforting the sick and dying was not suitable for Mendel's delicate disposition. Napp knew that the young monk was a gifted student and would make a good teacher while still performing other religious duties. When an opportunity came up for a seventh-grade teaching job in the nearby town of Znaim, Napp recommended Mendel for it.

Mendel took this new job in October of 1849. Although he did not have a teaching license, he was allowed to teach temporarily. In order to become a teacher permanently, Mendel had to obtain a license. He applied for permission to take the test and was accepted even though he did not have many university credits. Mendel studied for the exam while working twenty hours a week preparing lessons and performing monastery duties. He had to write two essays and take oral examinations. One of his written essays on geology was rejected for being unclear. The other had to do with meteorology, the properties of air, and the origin of wind. This essay was accepted. Mendel was so nervous during his oral examinations that he mumbled his way through them and gave unsatisfactory answers. He did not pass. He had no other choice but to study harder and take the test again.

Father Napp again came to Mendel's rescue. He sent Mendel to the University of Vienna to study natural history. In the 1800s, clerics, scientists, and intellectuals wanted to better understand how nature worked and how it fit into their religious beliefs. Mendel stayed there for almost two years studying biology, physics, and mathematics.

MENDEL ATTENDS THE UNIVERSITY OF VIENNA

The time he spent at the university prepared Mendel for his work in the field of science. He loved physics and math and enjoyed biology as well. Some of Mendel's teachers and friends were brilliant men. One such scientist was the Austrian physicist Christian Doppler, who discovered the Doppler effect. The Doppler effect is the change of frequency of

Christian Doppler was one of Mendel's teachers at the university.

sound waves that emanate from a moving object. For example, if a police car is parked by the side of a road and its siren is going, and you are standing nearby, you will hear the same sound frequency. If the police car moves toward or away from you, the frequency of the siren you hear will change.

When Mendel attended the University of Vienna, Doppler was the director of the Physical Institute. He hired Mendel as an assistant demonstrator at the institute even though all of twelve slots had already been filled. Doppler's ideas on experimental physics helped Mendel in his own plant experiments.

When Doppler died, another physicist named Andreas von Ettingshausen became the director of the Physical Institute. Mendel had yet another good teacher. He learned about Ettingshausen's combination theory, in which math is used to arrange groups of things, such as colors, flowers, and peas. Later, Mendel put the combination theory to use to help him in his own experiments with garden peas.

Another teacher who had a strong influence on Mendel was a German botanist named Franz Unger, who headed the

Mendel learned a lot about plants from Professor Franz Unger.

The University of Vienna

The University of Vienna was founded on March 12, 1365, by Duke Rudolf IV of Austria. For about twenty years, the university struggled to survive because of a lack of organization and funds. In the 1380s, Albert III, Rudolf's brother, asked educators in Paris, France, to help him restructure the school. Within ten years, the university was reorganized and had faculty members to teach theology, law, medicine, and philosophy. The university flourished until the early 1500s, when school officials declared that all students accept the Roman Catholic faith and the number of students attending the school declined.

By the time Gregor Mendel attended the university in the mid–1800s, the school had severed its ties with the Roman Catholic Church

plant physiology department at the university. He was an expert on plant cell life. Unger encouraged his students to study how plant cells divide and grow and to examine variations in plants and plant hybridization, or the process of breeding a plant using two different varieties. He talked about the pea plant and how easy it was to breed.

In the spring of 1854, Mendel returned to Brünn and began teaching at the new technical school there. His large classes of sixty to one hundred pupils were in science, physics, and natural history. Once again, this was a temporary teaching position because he had not received his permanent license. He also became a member of the new natural science section of Brünn's Agricultural Society.

and was self-governing. During the reign of Empress Maria Theresa in the 1700s, the university had undergone many positive changes. Departments of natural science and natural history were added as well as a chemistry professorship and an academy of sciences.

Mendel studied under such notable teachers as Christian Doppler and Karl von Littrow, a famous astronomer. Although Mendel never passed his oral teaching exams because of his extreme nervousness, he had the benefit of studying under some of the finest scientists of the day. The instruction Mendel received at the University of Vienna contributed to his own scientific exploration and data collecting skills.

Mendel became a popular teacher. His students found him patient, fair, and clear in his teaching methods. Although he was not a fashionable person, wearing his plain clothes and gold-rimmed glasses, he was a lively teacher who led interesting discussions. His intelligence and his interest in science were felt by his students.

In 1855, Mendel applied to take the teachers' examination a second time. He was accepted, but never completed the exam. His anxious and sensitive personality made him realize he would never be able to take the test. He did not work well under pressure. He liked to work alone and organize things. He also enjoyed teaching but was aware that he could only advance so far as a teacher if he didn't take and pass the exam. Mendel was allowed to continue teaching at half the regular teachers' pay because he wasn't certified.

This failure to receive his teaching license helped Mendel to direct his energies to the natural sciences. He wanted to study the workings of heredity and explore his ideas on sexual reproduction in animals and plants.

FOUR

From Mice to Peas

Mendel wanted to determine how traits were passed from parents to their offspring. He began his experiments with mice. He kept the mice in cages in his small apartment and bred them to see what would happen when white and brown mice mated. What colors would the babies be? Would they have coats with blended white and brown colors or coats that were all white or all brown? Mendel never found out the answers to these questions because the local bishop, Anton Ernst Schaffgotsch, did not approve of Mendel's breeding experiments. He thought studying the reproductive habits of mice was messy, smelly, and unsuitable for a monk. Mendel didn't want to stop his exploration of the topic, so he switched his experiments to the ordinary garden pea. Bishop

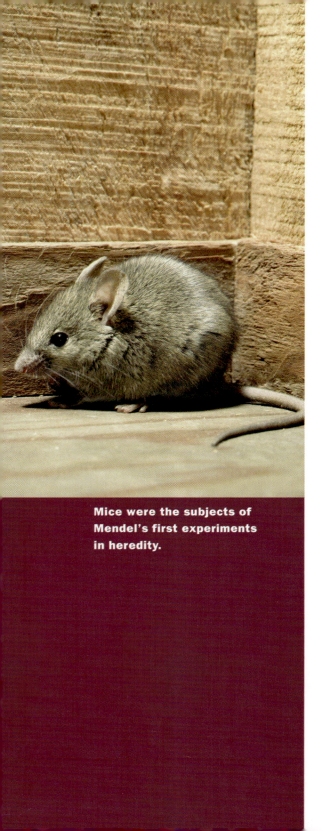

Mice were the subjects of Mendel's first experiments in heredity.

Schaffgotsch agreed to this change, and in 1854, Mendel started his pea experiments in the St. Thomas Monastery greenhouse, which was located in a corner of the courtyard. His goal was to observe how certain traits passed from generation to generation.

Mendel chose pea plants because he once said, "Preliminary experiments with the legume family showed that *Pisum sativum* had the right qualifications." He was right. The garden pea was a good experimental plant because he had access to several varieties that "bred true." That means the varieties consistently created offspring with the same characteristics. Another point was that the tight structure of the flower in which the reproductive organs are located prevents outside pollination unless artificial pollination is used. A third advantage was that peas come in many varieties with different, distinct traits, so Mendel could breed many combinations of parent plants.

EARLIER EXPERIMENTERS

Mendel was not the first scientist to conduct experiments in plant hybridization. In the late 1700s, a German scientist named Josef Kolreuter performed experiments that showed plants can self-pollinate as well as be fertilized by other plants. He also experimented in cross-pollination between plants and succeeded in breeding first and second generations of hybrids, or offspring of two parents with different traits. But he could not come to any final conclusions as to why some hybrid generations had inherited traits from other generations. He had not developed any laws of inheritance. Years later, another German scientist named Karl von Gärtner conducted his own plant experiments. He bred some 250 hybrid plants in close to ten thousand hybridization experiments. He even published a book called

Mendel decided to use the pea plant for his experiments.

Experiments and Observations of Hybridization in the Plant Kingdom. When he died, Gärtner had done considerable work in plant hybridization but had not developed any laws of inheritance that would explain how traits were passed from parent to offspring.

Kolreuter and Gärtner had offered valuable insights on how plants reproduce, but there was a difference between their work and Mendel's. Mendel would perform similar breeding experiments, but he would go further by recording and studying his results using a system of numbers and letters that would explain the basic laws of heredity.

GETTING STARTED

To begin his experiments, Mendel chose thirty-four different seed types that he tested for two years to make sure that they bred true. Mendel had to be certain that the offspring of a single parent plant that had a certain trait would consistently have offspring with that trait if allowed to self-pollinate. He knew that traits were passed on in pollen and eggs. For example, if one short parent plant self-pollinated, it should make only short plants. If one tall parent plant self-pollinated, it should make only tall plants. Every plant would show either of the two elements (now called genes) of the trait.

Mendel then selected twenty-two of these thirty-four true-breeding plants for fertilization. Now he was ready to begin the real work of cross-fertilizing these twenty-two plants and listing the traits of their offspring. He chose seven traits to study: seed shape, either smooth or wrinkled; seed color, either yellow or green; plant height, either tall or short; flower position, either flowers on the tip or near the stem; color of pods, either green or yellow; pod shape, either smooth or ridged; and seed coat color, either gray or white.

In the spring of 1856, Mendel was ready to plant the pea seeds in an outdoor garden. He was given a 23- by 115-foot (7- by 35-meter) plot in the monastery garden. It was originally thought that Mendel planted them in a small strip of land alongside the monastery, but other research showed that he probably planted his peas in a larger, sunnier place near the service entrance.

Mendel began his experiments by studying each characteristic separately. First, he chose two types of peas. One type produced smooth seeds and the other produced wrinkled seeds. In the late spring, when the smooth-seeded plants developed flowers, he hand-pollinated them with pollen from the wrinkle-seeded plants to make hybrids, or offspring of two parents that have different traits.

One of the seven traits that Mendel wanted to study was wrinkled or smooth seed shape.

Hand-pollination took lots of patience. Mendel usually did this work in the early morning, when the pollen was safe from wind and insects. With tweezers in hand, he walked from plant to plant, gently opening the two-part flower and finding the stamens, or male reproductive organs, that held the pollen. He snipped off the anthers, or pollen-bearing parts, and dropped the pollen bulbs into his robe pocket. Later, he used a small brush to dust the stigma, or sticky surface of the female reproductive system, with the desired pollen. A grain of pollen would travel down to the ovule and fertilize the egg. He put small cloth bags over the flowers to protect the pollen. He called the purebred, true-breeding, self-pollinated plants the P generation for "parental."

In the fall, the peas were ready to harvest. The pods were full and hard. When he opened the pea pods to look at the hybrid seeds, they were all smooth. What happened to the wrinkled seeds? Had they disappeared? If the parental traits had blended, as was thought at the time, the plants should have been partly wrinkled and partly smooth, but they weren't. He called the first generation of these plants F1, for "first filial" generation (from the Latin word *filius*, which means "son").

The following spring, he planted the hybrid seeds. This time, he let the peas self-pollinate. The pollen from a flower would fertilize an egg from the same plant. When the plants ripened, he opened the seed pods and found both wrinkled and smooth seeds in the second-generation plants. He counted 7,324 seeds from 253 hybrids of which 5,474 were smooth and 1,850 were wrinkled. This gave him a ratio of 2.96:1 or three smooth seeds to one wrinkled seed. Mendel discovered that the

It is thought that Mendel may have used this garden space at the monastery for his experiments.

wrinkled element of the seed shape had been hidden for a generation before returning in the next generation. He deduced that there must be two factors, one donated by each parent, that determined seed shape. Because the wrinkled trait had remained hidden for a generation but then reappeared, he called the element that caused the wrinkled trait "recessive." Some of the seeds were always smooth, so he called the element that caused the smooth trait the dominating one. ("Dominating" was later changed to the term "dominant.") He also saw that the two traits had not blended in individual seeds. The seeds were either smooth or wrinkled, not partly smooth and partly wrinkled. His experiments showed him that each plant had two units of heredity. Some of the pollen carried the dominant unit and some carried a recessive unit. The eggs also had either the dominant unit or the recessive unit. Today, these units of heredity are known as genes.

Mendel then went on to study the other six traits of garden peas using the same method he had used in his first experiment. When he counted the peas, he found he always came up with a ratio of three to one. This meant that he found that three times as many offspring with dominant traits as recessive ones in the F2 generation. He used a capital letter to describe the dominating element and a lowercase letter to show the recessive element. A plant with two dominating elements would be represented as AA and a plant with a dominating and a recessive element would be represented as Aa. Mendel saw that when the hybrids were crossed there were different seed combinations. The possible combinations were AA, aA, Aa, and aa. Because he saw a ratio of three dominant (A) to one recessive (a) traits in the offspring, he concluded that only plants with two recessive genes (aa) would display the recessive trait.

Mendel was then curious to see what would happen when he cross-fertilized plants with two different traits. He crossed plants that had smooth yellow seeds with plants that had wrinkled green seeds. The first generation produced only smooth yellow seeds, the dominant form. Then Mendel let these hybrid offspring self-pollinate. When the pods were ready for picking, he shelled them and counted the peas. Out of 556 seeds, he counted 315 smooth and yellow, 108 smooth and green, 101 wrinkled and yellow, and 32 wrinkled and green. There were four different combinations. The ratio was 9:3:3:1. This means that out of sixteen possible offspring combinations, nine had yellow smooth seeds, three had yellow wrinkled seeds, three had smooth green seeds, and one had green wrinkled seeds.

Phenotype and Genotype

Wilhelm Johannsen, a professor of plant physiology at Copenhagen Agricultural College in Denmark, developed the scientific words called "phenotype" and "genotype." Phenotype comes from the Greek word *phainein*, or to show. It refers to how something looks, or its appearance. Genotype comes from the word *gene* and describes the makeup of a living organism, or what genes it has. Only peas with two recessive traits, genotype aa, would have the recessive phenotype.

Mendel's First Law

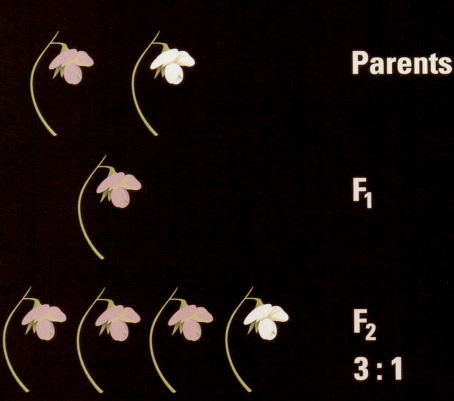

Parents

F₁

F₂
3 : 1

Mendel's law of segregation proved that alleles (different forms of the same gene for a specific trait) segregate, or separate, during the formation of reproductive cells. Therefore, though dominant traits prevail, a recessive trait of one of the parents will show up in an F2 generation in a ratio of 3:1.

MENDEL'S RESULTS

After growing nearly thirty thousand plants and studying the results of all seven traits of peas over a period of eight years, Mendel concluded that the information stored in the pollen and egg cell determined the different elements that were passed on to offspring. He proposed that these elements were independent of each other and were passed on as individual units in a predictable and precise way. He developed these ideas into two important rules of heredity.

The first law was the principle of segregation. This law states that an egg or pollen transmits information that codes for one form of a specific trait. That is, each pollen and egg cell carries half the information that determines the phenotype and genotype of the offspring. For example, in the case of peas, one form of the trait codes for smooth seeds, and the other form codes for wrinkled seeds.

Linkage

Linkage occurs when two or more genes are often inherited as a group because they are located close to each other on a chromosome, or structure within a cell that carries genetic information. Mendel was not aware of this during his experiments. Later research showed that even though gene linkage occurred, sometimes the linked genes separated from each other in future generations. Linkage helped scientists find the location of genes on chromosomes.

The second law is the principle of independent assortment of traits. Mendel thought that these inherited elements were passed on separately and didn't affect one another. One element could determine hair color and another eye color. Later, the discovery of linkage would require Mendel's law of independent assortment to be amended.

Mendel had finally found his place in the world. He was conducting important experiments and teaching classes at the Brünn Technical Institute, where he was a popular teacher. He had the security, privacy, and support of the monastery, which allowed him to continue his scientific exploration. Now all he had to do was convince other scientists of the value of his work.

FIVE

My Time Will Come

While Mendel was toiling in his garden, another scientist and naturalist named Charles Darwin was conducting important scientific research. He had traveled to South America and was amazed at the varieties of life-forms he found there. After many years of traveling and studying the traits and behaviors of life-forms, Darwin began to wonder why some of these organisms flourished and reproduced, while others had disappeared. He wrote a book on his ideas called *On the Origin of Species by Means of Natural Selection*. It was published in 1859, a few years before Mendel finished his pea experiments.

Darwin believed that living things were always changing slowly, or evolving, over time. Organisms that were well-suited to their environment

Charles Darwin was an important naturalist who revolutionized the field of biology with his theories.

survived. Those that were not died or had fewer offspring. He called this theory survival of the fittest, or natural selection. He believed that in order for a species to survive, they had to adapt to changing climates, food sources, and predators. He used the term variation to describe animals and plants that reproduce offspring in one generation, which are similar to the second generation, but not exact copies of their parents. Some other variations are caused by gene mutations that can be passed

Two Important Scientists Who Never Met

Gregor Mendel and Charles Darwin are two men who should have met each other. They could have shared their unique ideas on how life evolves, adapts, and changes. Gregor Mendel was curious about how character traits were transferred from parent to offspring. Darwin also wanted to know how this happened, but he didn't test his ideas through scientific methods and then record and analyze his findings. Mendel suggested that elements (genes) within the plant cells were responsible for passing on certain traits. Darwin had his own theory, which he called pangenesis. He thought the body released invisible particles he called gemmules that blended together to create new life and were passed on to the new generation through fertilization. Darwin never proved his theory, because he didn't perform experiments and present clear results. Mendel set out to explain his theories and presented them in a paper to the scientific community.

on to offspring. Other variations are produced by changes in the environment and are not passed on by parents to their offspring. Useful variations make certain organisms better adapted to their environments, making it more likely that the organisms will live longer and have more opportunities to reproduce and pass on these useful traits.

Darwin believed in a blending theory of inheritance, in which traits from both parents were mixed together in the offspring. But Mendel showed in his pea experiments that traits were passed on independently from one generation to another. Peas had either a yellow or green color, not a blending of yellow and green. Unfortunately, Darwin was unaware of Mendel's experiments.

MENDEL'S RESEARCH PAPER

In 1863, Mendel finished his pea experiments and prepared to share his findings with the scientific community. For two years, he had spent many hours in the monastery library, organizing his notebooks and writing the paper he planned to present to an association called the Natural Sciences Society of Brünn. He knew it would be a challenge to convince his fellow scientists of his discoveries. For years, many of his colleagues had questions about heredity. Many experiments, discussions, and research papers had been conducted by them. Mendel had even studied many of these earlier scientific efforts and had added the results or observations of these experiments to his own knowledge about hybridization. But no one had developed any specific laws to explain how parents passed on traits to

The Linnaean System

In the 1730s, Karl von Linné, a Swedish botanist (he wrote under the Latin version of his name, Carolus Linnaeus) developed a system called binomial nonenclature that categorized all living things based on their similarities. He divided organisms into two kingdoms, plant and animal. Then, he divided these kingdoms into classes, orders, genera, and species. Each organism has a scientific name. For example, the scientific name for the house cat is *Felis domesticus*. The genus name is *Felis*. A genus name refers to a group of closely related species. *Domesticus* is the species name. A species is a group of organisms that have similar traits and are able to interbreed. Binomial nonenclature helped scientists such as Mendel determine the closest relatives of peas and how many different species of peas there were. The system is still used today.

their offspring until Mendel applied his mathematical and analytical skills to the problem.

    Mendel had devised a system to document his pea plant crossbreeding results. He used a single letter to represent a dominant and a recessive element. A capital letter represented dominant and the same lowercase letter represented recessive. A plant that had two dominant elements would show the dominant trait. A plant that had two recessive element would show the recessive trait.

This is a page from Mendel's paper. It is possible to see his method for representing dominant and recessive elements.

Pollenzellen   *A*   *A*   *a*   *a*

Keimzellen   *A*   *A*   *a*   *a*

Das Ergebniss der Befruchtung lässt sich dadurch anschaulich machen, dass die Bezeichnungen für die verbundenen Keim- und Pollenzellen in Bruchform angesetzt werden, und zwar für die Pollenzellen über, für die Keimzellen unter dem Striche. Man erhält in dem vorliegenden Falle:

$$\frac{A}{A} + \frac{A}{a} + \frac{a}{A} + \frac{a}{a}$$

Bei dem ersten und vierten Gliede sind Keim- und Pollenzellen gleichartig, daher müssen die Producte ihrer Verbindung constant sein, nämlich *A* und *a*; bei dem zweiten und dritten hingegen erfolgt abermals eine Vereinigung der beiden differirenden Stamm-Merkmale, daher auch die aus diesen Befruchtungen hervorgehenden Formen mit der Hybride, von welcher sie abstammen, ganz identisch sind. Es findet demnach eine wiederholte Hybridisirung statt. Daraus erklärt sich die auffallende Erscheinung, dass die Hybriden im Stande sind, nebst den beiden Stammformen auch Nachkommen zu erzeugen, die ihnen selbst gleich sind; $\frac{A}{a}$ und $\frac{a}{A}$ geben beide dieselbe Verbindung *Aa*, da es, wie schon früher angeführt wurde, für den Erfolg der Befruchtung keinen Unterschied macht, welches von den beiden Merkmalen der Pollen- oder Keimzelle angehört. Es ist daher

$$\frac{A}{A} + \frac{A}{a} + \frac{a}{A} + \frac{a}{a} = A + 2 Aa + a.$$

So gestaltet sich der mittlere Verlauf bei der Selbstbefruchtung der Hybriden, wenn in denselben zwei differirende Merkmale vereinigt sind. In einzelnen Blüthen und an einzelnen Pflanzen kann jedoch das Verhältniss, in welchem die Formen der Reihe gebildet werden, nicht unbedeutende Störungen erleiden. Abgesehen davon, dass die Anzahl, in welcher beiderlei Keimzellen im Fruchtknoten vorkommen, nur im Durchschnitte als gleich angenommen werden kann, bleibt es ganz dem Zufalle überlassen, welche von den beiden Pollenarten an jeder einzelnen Keimzelle die Befruchtung vollzieht. Desshalb müs-

It wasn't easy for people to understand Mendel's findings because he used mathematical equations to explain them. It wasn't until the early 1900s when another scientist developed a way to present a clearer picture of the results of Mendel's crossbreeding experiments by developing something called the Punnett square.

On a cold winter day in February of 1865, Mendel was ready to share his findings. He had spent years planting, crossbreeding, and recording his results. He hoped that the distinguished men who had come to hear his paper would understand the methods and numbers he used to record the results of his work.

Nervously, he stood in front of the Natural Sciences Society of Brünn. His appearance and clothing were simple. He was a short, plump man, dressed in an ankle-length, long-sleeved black garment with a tunic over it

The Punnett Square

Reginald Crundall Punnett, a zoologist at Cambridge University, came up with a clearer model to show Mendel's pea plant results. Punnett devised a checkerboard diagram to record the crossings Mendel had described in his scientific paper. The diagram clearly shows the possible genotypes of offspring produced sexually using Mendel's letter notations of a capital letter for a dominant trait and a lowercase letter for a recessive trait. The Punnett square was a visual tool Mendel did not use when presenting his findings. If he had, it might have helped his fellow scientists better appreciate his work.

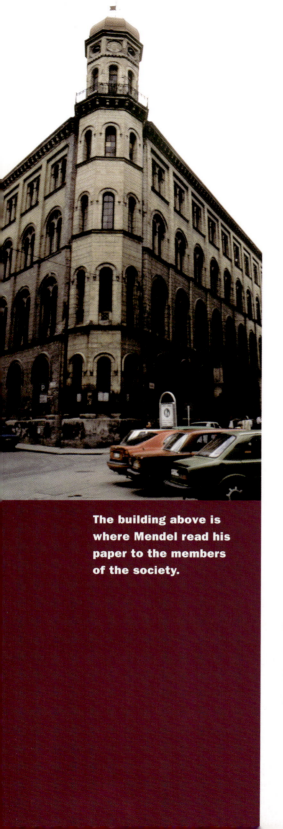

The building above is where Mendel read his paper to the members of the society.

that was belted at the waist. He had with him a few pea plants and his paper. The audience before him numbered about forty scientists. Many of them were members and honorary members of the society. Mendel took a deep breath. He was going to talk about peas, "his children," *Pisum sativum*.

The quiet, studious monk began to speak. Everyone appeared to be listening. After an hour, he finished and eagerly waited for questions, but there were only some general comments, not a single question. The meeting ended and Mendel left, disappointed with the lack of interest in his paper. He wondered if anyone understood what he had just said.

Four weeks later, Mendel appeared a second time before the Natural Sciences Society and read the second half of his paper. Once again, there were no questions. Mendel was beginning to think his two talks had been too difficult for the audience to comprehend. He had shown the results of his pea plant experiments using a mathematical system that may have been too complicated for the audience to grasp. Whatever the reasons were, Mendel was disappointed at the lack of response his paper had received, but he wasn't discouraged. He said to a friend, "My time will come."

In 1866, Mendel followed up his speech with the publication of his paper in the Brünn society's official journal. His paper was printed under the title "Experiments on Plant Hybridization." It was published in German. Mendel ordered forty copies of the article to be printed and wrote an introductory letter. He mailed the letters out to botanists, biologists, and other professional people, including Charles Darwin. If members of the scientific community hadn't paid attention to his speech, maybe they would give his work a second chance if they saw it in written form.

MENDEL, PROFESSOR NÄGELI, AND HAWKWEED

In December of 1866, Professor Karl von Nägeli of the University of Munich received a reprint of Mendel's scientific paper along with a letter describing his eight years of experiments. Von Nägeli was interested in Mendel's paper because he was also experimenting with crossbreeding a plant called *Hieracium*, also known as hawkweed.

Karl von Nägeli was the only person who showed interest in Mendel's scientific findings.

In February of 1867, Mendel received a response to his paper. A letter arrived from Karl von Nägeli. He was polite in his comments and even understood Mendel's complicated equations, but von Nägeli was skeptical about Mendel's notions of dominance and principle of segregation. He thought Mendel's ratio of three to one might hold true for pea plants, but that information was not enough to prove that Mendel's laws of inheritance were correct. Von Nägeli had his own ideas about inheritance. He believed that offspring acquired some hereditary information from the mother and some from the father, and there was a blending of traits. Mendel didn't believe in the blending of traits. His experiments had show that traits were inherited independently of each other, and that some traits disappeared for a generation, only to resurface in the next generation.

Mendel didn't know exactly what the elements were. Later research revealed that elements (genes) were composed of deoxyribonucleic acid (DNA), which contains chemical codes that determine traits.

Mendel wrote back to von Nägeli defending his experiments by saying he believed that at least some of his hybrids would always breed true. His experiments showed that the parents' genes were separate and unchanged and were passed independently from each other. Pairs of different traits were independent units that were dominant or recessive and passed on intact from parent to offspring. This proved to him that there wasn't any blending or mixing of traits.

Over the next seven years, Mendel and von Nägeli corresponded with each other. In one of the early letters, Mendel offered to help von

Nägeli with his hawkweed experiments. Mendel asked the professor to send him some seeds so he could try to crossbreed the plants. Von Nägeli agreed, but hawkweed proved to be a difficult plant to hybridize. The flowers were slippery and very small, and Mendel had to use a microscope to pull the fragile flowers apart. The work was tiresome, and eventually, his eyesight suffered. He continued experimenting with the hawkweed for five years, but never achieved results that were successful.

ABBOT MENDEL

Mendel's position in the St. Thomas Monastery changed. On March 30, 1868, Mendel was elected to be the new abbot of the monastery. Abbot Napp had died a year earlier. Mendel competed against another monk named Anselm Rambousek for the position. It was a close race, but Mendel had the

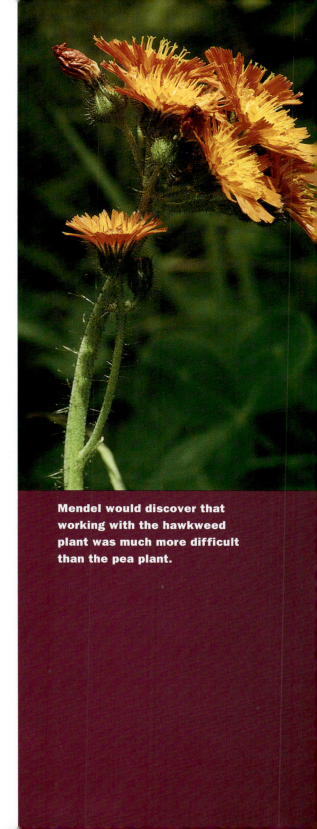

Mendel would discover that working with the hawkweed plant was much more difficult than the pea plant.

right qualifications. He was liked by the other monks, was of German heritage, and could speak both German and Czech. There was a national Czech movement going on at this time, but the Hapsburg monarchy supported its German roots.

After accepting his new job, Mendel continued with the delicate and difficult hawkweed experiments, but with little success. He was only able to obtain a few hybrid seeds. Mendel and von Nägeli did not know that hawkweed could produce seeds without pollination. The plants reproduced asexually. The seeds came from the egg cells within the plant. Instead of inheriting traits from two parents, the plant's offspring were identical copies of the mother plants. Therefore, hybrids were rare.

With all the responsibilities of his new position, Mendel found it too difficult to continue with his plant research.

Doctor Miescher and DNA

In 1869, four years after Mendel published his paper on the pea experiments, a Swiss doctor named Johann Friedrich Miescher discovered a substance in the nucleus, or central part, of the white blood cell. He called this material "nucleic acid" and thought that the proteins in this acid might be the key to heredity. He needed lots of white blood cells to examine this material, so he collected the pus-covered bandages of wounded soldiers recuperating in hospitals. Miescher didn't know that DNA was present in the nucleic acid. It wasn't until the 1900s when another scientist isolated DNA that the importance of Miescher's discovery became apparent.

Eventually, Mendel suffered serious eyestrain caused by using very fine needles, a microscope, and a magnifying glass to crossbreed the difficult hawkweed. His bad eyesight, in addition to his new duties, forced him to stop the experiments. After a year, he went back to the work and wrote a paper called "On Hieracium—Hybrids Obtained by Artificial Fertilization." In June of 1869, he gave a lecture on the paper at the Natural Sciences Society of Brünn. A year later, the paper was published.

Mendel's new position as abbot took up so much of his time and energy that he could not teach or spend long hours working on the mystery of how hawkweed plants inherited traits. He decided to stop the plant work and gave up his teaching position at Brünn's Modern School. He wrote to Professor von Nägeli, "I find myself moved into a sphere, place, in which much appears strange to me, and it will take some time and effort before I feel at home in it."

Robert Hooke and the Discovery of Cells

In the mid-1600s, an Englishman named Robert Hooke built the first compound microscope (using more than one lens) to study minute things, such as the eye of a fly, the silverfish, the life cycle of mosquitoes, and the structure of bird feathers. He also observed slices of plant stems, wood, and cork. Hooke made one of his most important discoveries while studying cork under his microscope. He noticed that the cork was made up of thousands of tiny chambers resembling small boxes or compartments. He called these chambers "cells" because they looked like small rooms. Hooke recorded his observations of the cellular structure of living tissue. He then published his findings in a book called *Micrographia*. Hooke was the first person to describe cells, although he had no knowledge of the internal structure of the cell that held the secrets of how traits are passed from generation to generation.

Gregor Mendel's life had taken a new path. His work as a scientist was no longer a priority. Whatever contributions he had made to the scientific community now rested in their hands. He had only to wait for recognition.

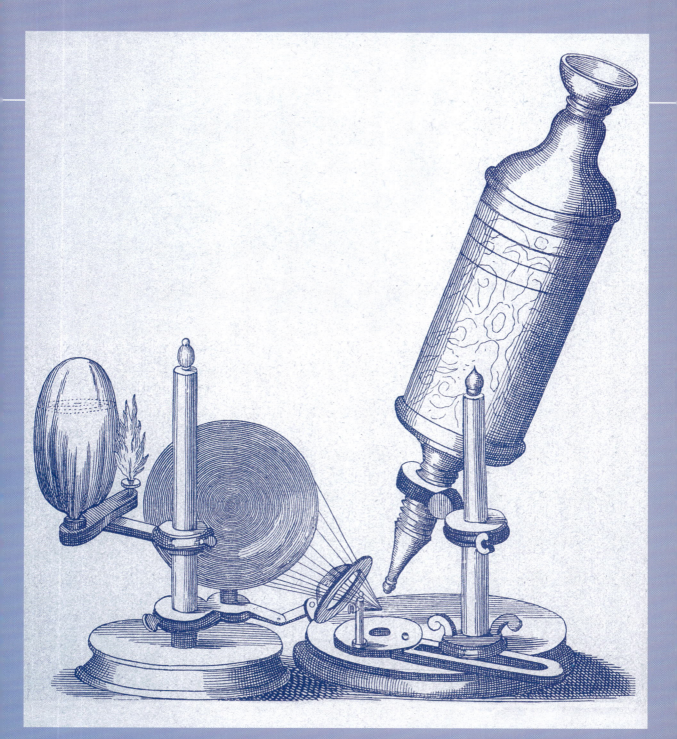

SIX

Abbot Mendel

Gregor Mendel was forty-six years old when he became the abbot of the St. Thomas Monastery. His appointment was approved by the German emperor and his fellow German and Czech monks. For the next sixteen years of his life, Mendel held this important position.

There were benefits to being abbot of the monastery. He moved into new, larger rooms and received a handsome salary. Because he had no use for the money himself, he was able to help his sister Theresia and her three sons, Johann, Alois, and Ferdinand. He paid school tuition for all three boys. Two became doctors and one became a teacher. He also gave money to the needy in the Brünn community and sent money to his home village to help develop a fire department.

Abbot Mendel was happy to be of service to so many people. His numerous responsibilities included heading organizations and societies, such as the Agricultural Society of Moravia; entertaining dignitaries and visitors to the monastery; and watching over the monastery's lands. He also traveled to Berlin, Vienna, and Rome on official duties.

Mendel was very generous with his family and the community. This is the fire station that Mendel helped pay for.

Although Mendel was busy being abbot, he still found time for gardening. He liked to plant fruit trees and had many varieties in the monastery garden. He also enjoyed growing flowers and particularly liked the fuchsia flower with its bell-shaped flowers in colors of purple, white, pink, and red. He also renewed his interest in bees. He kept swarms of different varieties of bees and gave every hive a number. He wanted to crossbreed different kinds of bees to optimize honey production. But Mendel soon found out that crossbreeding bees was difficult. The queen bee and the drones were very particular and didn't seem to like mating in a box. He did finally succeed in crossbreeding, but his increasing responsibilities as abbot forced him to end his bee work.

MENDEL THE WEATHERMAN

Mendel had another interest besides gardening and beekeeping. For many years, he had been a student of meteorology, which is the scientific study of weather. From 1848 to 1862, he compiled weather information on temperature, wind speed, air pressure, moisture, and rain and snowfall amounts using a weather compass. He made many graphs and charts to record how weather patterns changed over the years. In 1863, The Natural Sciences Society of Brünn published his report of weather information in its journal and had copies made for people interested in meteorology.

During this period, the study of weather was a fairly new science. It had begun in Italy in the 1500s when instruments were developed to measure the temperature, air pressure, and moisture content. The first thermometer was made by the astronomer Galileo, and an instrument called a barometer, which measured air pressure, was invented by a scientist named Torricelli.

On October 13, 1870, Abbot Mendel experienced a scary and exciting weather event when a tornado passed through Brünn. Mendel was in his room when he heard a thundering noise. The sky became very dark, and a wind stronger than any he had ever felt whipped against the monastery walls. The windows shattered, and roof tiles went flying into

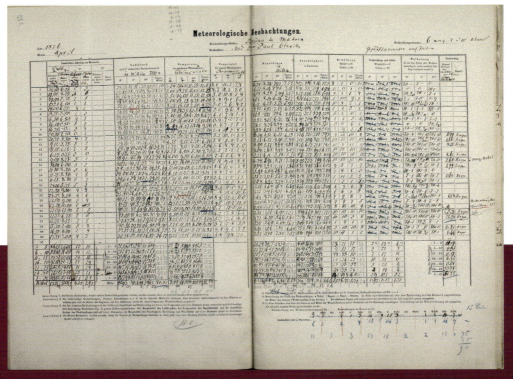

These are some notes on the weather taken by Mendel.

Mendel's room. When things calmed down, he watched the big funnel of wind leave as quickly as it had arrived. He realized he had experienced the devastating effects of a tornado.

His scientific mind took over, and Mendel started to study the forces that caused tornadoes. He wrote a research paper titled "The Whirlwind of October 13, 1870" and gave a talk at the Natural Sciences Society. He also wrote another paper called "The Foundation for Weather Forecasting." He also became Brünn's official weather-watcher when the previous one became ill. Mendel recorded the weather three times a day and sent the information to the central weather station in Vienna.

MENDEL THE POLITICIAN

In 1874, Mendel became a political activist. Although Mendel had always been a quiet, gentle man who did not like conflicts, he found himself involved in a political struggle with the Hapsburg government about taxes.

Each time a new abbot was elected, a high property tax was levied on the monastery, even though the monastery never paid any other taxes. In 1874, the Austro-Hungarian Empire, demanded that all the monasteries in Brünn pay a city tax of 36,680 guilders for the next five years to a state-run religious fund to help support parish priests. Mendel thought this was wrong. He began a long letter-writing campaign to fight the tax. After all, Mendel argued, the monastery provided many

Mendel's Tornado

When Mendel experienced one of nature's most powerful weather events, very little was known about tornadoes (also known as cyclones or twisters). Although tornadoes occur around the world, Brünn's storm was an unusual event. Mendel watched in awe as a massive column of furiously swirling wind whipped into the St. Thomas Monastery's courtyard. The force of the violent storm sent tree branches, parts of buildings, and roof tiles in all directions. Windows were smashed, and the monastery's greenhouse was destroyed. Mendel estimated the tornado lasted no longer than five seconds, but he used his weather observation skills to remember what he saw. Later on, he wrote a scientific paper on this unforgettable force of nature. He presented this paper to the Natural Sciences Society of Brünn in November of the same year.

Although Mendel wrote a detailed paper describing what he had seen, the causes of tornadoes and their levels of intensity were unknown. Today, scientists can measure the strength of tornadoes by using the Fujita-Pearson Tornado Intensity Scale, which rates tornadoes on a scale from F0 to F5. The numbers represent the power of a tornado by looking at the damage it caused to buildings, trees, and other human-made and natural structures.

services to the community. He argued that his monastery could pay 2,000 guilders, but that 36,680 guilders was too much to ask from a religious organization. He sent his letters to the government, the ministry of education, the tax collector, and to any other organization that would listen to him.

Mendel's political views caused controversy within the church. He spoke in favor of the Liberal Party, not the Conservative National Party, which the Catholic Church favored. Mendel supported the Liberal Party's policy of equal rights for ethnic Czechs, not only for German and Hungarian groups. People were surprised that this shy, nervous abbot was being so outspoken. Many of them couldn't understand why he was fighting so hard against the taxes when everyone else was paying them. But Mendel firmly believed that these taxes were unfair. In spite of his opposition to the taxes, the government took over part of the monastery's properties to pay for its overdue taxes. Mendel continued his fight for ten long years. The battle caused Mendel to suffer nervous

Francis Joseph was the emperor of Austria and the king of Hungary in the 1800s.

exhaustion. He began to distrust people and preferred to be alone. His only relaxation came from his hobbies.

ILLNESS AND DEATH

In the summer of 1883, Mendel's health began to decline. He had suffered from kidney problems for many years, but as he grew older, his condition became worse. He developed Bright's disease, which is called nephritis today. The disease causes the kidneys to become inflamed and can cause kidney failure. In addition, he had become obese and had

The Hapsburg Empire

In the early 1500s, the Ottoman Turks invaded central Europe. King Lajos II of Hungary and Bohemia died while fighting the Turks. In order to prevent the conquest of Bohemia, the government accepted the help of the Austrian Hapsburg Empire, which then ruled over these lands for more than three hundred years. In the 1700s, the Hapsburg Empire controlled Bohemia and Moravia from its capital in Vienna, Austria. The population of these two areas was a combination of German and Czech. Mendel grew up in a German-speaking region, but he also learned the Czech language. The Hapsburgs wanted German to become the official language of the empire and forced the Czech population to speak and write in German.

developed a habit of smoking cigars. His nephews knew their uncle was sick, but they couldn't do anything other than visit and spend time with him. They lived near the monastery while attending school and often visited him on Sunday afternoons to play checkers, walk in the gardens, or just talk.

On January 4, 1884, Abbot Gregor Mendel died. He was sixty-one years old. He was given a respectful funeral and buried in the monastery tomb. A monk in the monastery wrote this poem about Mendel.

> Gentle, free-handed, kindly to one and all,
> Both brother and father to us brethren was he.
> Flowers he loved, and as a defender of the law he held
> out against injustice.
> Whereby at length worn out he died from a wound of
> the heart.

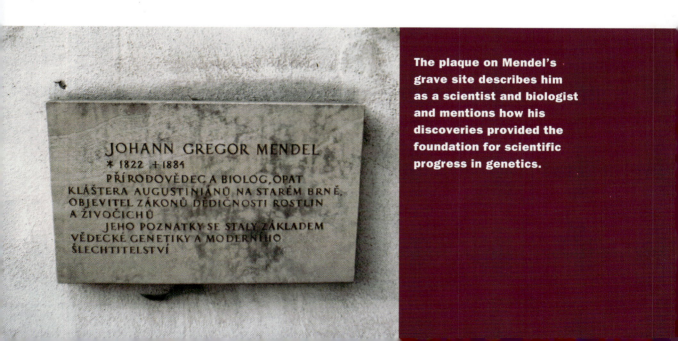

The plaque on Mendel's grave site describes him as a scientist and biologist and mentions how his discoveries provided the foundation for scientific progress in genetics.

Many kind words were written about the work he had done as a member of the St. Thomas Monastery and his interests in beekeeping, gardening, and weather watching. He was remembered as a religious man who enjoyed science and had many hobbies, but his most important contribution to science and the study of genetics remained unmentioned by natural historians and scientists.

After his death, most of Mendel's personal and scientific papers were burned on the order of his successor, Abbot Anselm Rambousek. Mendel's paper describing the pea experiments survived only because it had been sent out to other scientists. It is known that Mendel sent Charles Darwin a copy of his paper, but it remained unread. Ironically, Rambousek managed to get the government to stop collecting taxes and send the monastery a check for taxes it had paid. He had succeeded where Mendel had failed in ten long years of fighting with the government, but Mendel's true recognition would come in another way. The time would come when the scientific community finally realized what a valuable contribution this Augustinian monk and abbot had made to the world.

SEVEN

Mendel's Second Chance

In 1900, sixteen years after Mendel's death, three scientists independently rediscovered Mendel's important scientific paper on plant hybrids. One was Hugo de Vries, a Dutch biologist, who had done his own plant experiments in the late 1800s. Based on Mendel's work and his own plant experiments, de Vries wrote a paper on his theory of how traits passed from generation to generation. He cited Mendel's important contributions in his paper.

De Vries believed that something within living cells carried information about heredity. He called these units of heredity "pangens," and

his theory of inheritance was called "intracellular pangenesis" ("intracellular" means "inside the cell"). Pangenesis was the name given to Charles
Darwin's ideas on heredity. Darwin thought that every cell in the body gave

Hugo de Vries rediscovered Mendel's work after it had been ignored for years.

out tiny particles that moved through the body and settled in the eggs or sperm. These particles were then passed on from parent to offspring.

Another scientist who rediscovered Mendel's paper was Karl Correns, a German botanist who was doing research on hybrids in maize plants. Correns had studied with Karl von Nägeli, the scientist Mendel had tried to help with the fertilization of hawkweed plants. After Correns read Mendel's paper, he said, "Mendel's paper is one of the best ever written on hybrids." He then published his own paper called "Mendel's law concerning the behavior of progeny of varietal hybrids."

A third scientist named Erich von Tschermak was also conducting his own pea plant and flower experiments when he came across Mendel's paper. Like Correns, he began breeding peas in the late 1800s. In 1900, after doing further research in the field of heredity, he published a paper in an Austrian scientific journal on crossbreeding in pea plants. Von Tschermak also mentioned Mendel's work in his article.

Although these three men had done their own experiments in plant hybridization, they could not claim to be the first scientists to explain how traits are passed from parent to offspring. They had to accept the fact that an obscure Augustinian monk had already made this important discovery nearly fifty years earlier.

THOMAS MORGAN AND FRUIT FLIES

As soon as Mendel's work was rediscovered, it was challenged by scientists. They gave him credit for the work he had done, but some of them questioned his inheritance laws. One man who did not subscribe to the Mendelian laws of heredity was Thomas Hunt Morgan, an American researcher who was involved in important work with the fruit fly (*Drosophila melanogaster*) at Columbia University. Morgan was studying the breeding habits of the fruit fly in an effort to understand how mutations occur. The fruit fly was an excellent subject because it only had

Thomas Hunt Morgan did not believe in Mendel's theories and conducted studies with fruit flies to explore genetic mutations.

eight large chromosomes (two pairs of four) that were easy to see under early microscopes. In addition, fruit flies can produce hundreds of babies at a time. They're very small, so they don't take up a lot of space and don't need much food to live. Morgan bred the flies in empty milk bottles and fed them over-ripe bananas. His small laboratory quickly became known as the "fly room."

Morgan was looking to create mutations, or changes, in the flies by exposing them to chemicals and X-rays. For two years, there were no changes in the flies, but then one white-eyed male was born (all the fruit flies had red eyes). He bred the white-eyed male with a red-eyed female. There were more than twelve hundred offspring in the first generation, and they all had red eyes. This showed that Mendel's dominant trait theory was correct and that the recessive white-eyed trait had been masked.

Discovery of Chromosomes

In the late 1800s, a German biologist named Walther Flemming was studying living cells by using dyes. He saw that just before a cell divides to form two cells (mitosis), the dye is absorbed into the nucleus by a rod-shaped material he named chromatin. Flemming later named the threadlike material "chromosome" from the Greek words for "colored bodies." Chromosomes carry genes in the nucleus of every cell. Most cells contain two matching sets of genes. One set of genes is passed from each parent during reproduction. Genes are what determine such traits as eye and hair color.

Then Morgan crossbred the red-eyed hybrids with each other. The second generation showed that Mendel's law of segregation was also correct.

Jumping Genes

Believe it not, genes can actually jump from one place to another on a chromosome. These genes can place themselves into different parts of a chromosome and turn the genes near them on and off. In the 1940s, a scientist named Barbara McClintock noticed in her research on corn that certain corn kernels were speckled. Because corn kernel cells have the same genotype, or genetic makeup, McClintock wanted to find out why all the kernels weren't one color. She made an important discovery that encouraged a new way of thinking about deoxyribonucleic acid, or DNA, which carries the genetic code that gives every organism its characteristics. The genes were transposing themselves, or moving from one place to another on a chromosome. The idea that bits of DNA were leaving their original locations and inserting themselves elsewhere made scientists take a closer look at jumping genes and how mutations, or changes, can occur. McClintock provided evidence about her theory of transposons (commonly called "jumping genes"). At the time of her discovery, however, the scientific community was not impressed. It wasn't until the mid-1970s, when advancements in molecular biology allowed scientists to look for jumping genes, that her work was appreciated. These genes were found in bacteria, mammals, insects, and humans. Barbara McClintock was recognized for her jumping genes discovery in 1983 when she was awarded the Nobel Prize for science.

There was a ratio of three red-eyed flies to one white-eyed fly. But Morgan noticed something that would change Mendel's second law. All the female flies had red eyes, while all the males had white eyes. Morgan called this white-eyed trait a mutation. Further research showed that the gene for eye color was located on the X chromosome. Because female fruit flies had two X chromosomes, the dominant gene for red eyes was expressed. The male flies, however, had only one X chromosome, so if they inherited one with the recessive gene for white eyes, they had white eyes. This was the first time a certain gene had been located on a certain chromosome. Morgan had discovered sex linkage. Linkage can also occur when two or more genes are very close to each other on the same chromosome and are often inherited together. Therefore, Mendel's second law of independent assortment had to be amended.

Several years later, one of Morgan's students, A. H. Sturtevant, refined the linkage discovery. He examined several genes to see if they remained linked together as they passed from generation to generation. He found that genes that traveled together were located close together on the same chromosome. Genes that did not travel together were located farther apart on the chromosome. Sturtevant also saw that Mendel's law of independent assortment of traits, which said genes were independent of each other, was not totally correct. Genes that are inherited independently are located on different chromosomes or are located far apart on the same chromosome. Mendel had not noticed this important difference. Based on this new information, Sturtevant began to build a linkage map that showed how different genes moved together and were passed on to future generations. Gene mapping became a valuable tool in genetics.

MENDEL'S CHAMPION

William Bateson was another scientist who believed in Mendel's laws of inheritance. Bateson was looking for information about how new species arise, how crossbreeding works, and how it can be studied and recorded. He had read De Vries's paper on hybridizing monstrosities and was impressed with De Vries's theory of mutation. This paper stated that new species were not created gradually by an accumulation of small changes over time, but that they were created all at once. De Vries was also interested in Bateson's paper on how new species derive from hybridization.

The First Inherited Disease

The first inherited disease was discovered in 1902 by a Briton named Dr. Archibald Garrod. He noticed that a disorder called alkaptonuria caused urine to turn black after a person ate certain foods. It was a harmless disease, but Garrod showed that it was caused by an inherited trait. Because genes made proteins, and in alkaptonuria, a protein was not working properly, this defect could be passed onto offspring.

Bateson discovered Mendel's work while he was a lecturer at Cambridge University. When he read Mendel's paper "Experiments in Hybridization," it was as though lightning had hit him. The answers he had been searching for were in Mendel's laws of segregation and independent assortment. From that moment, he became Mendel's chief supporter and protector. He had Mendel's paper translated into English and published in 1902. He also added a preface called "Mendel's Principles of Heredity: A Defence." Bateson gave generously of his time and scientific knowledge to promote Mendel's theory of inheritance.

In the early 1900s, Bateson met Thomas Hunt Morgan. At that point, Morgan was not a believer in the Mendelian laws of heredity. Later, after he had done his fruit fly research, he wrote a book called *The Mechanism of Mendelian Heredity*, which explained that for the most part, Mendel's laws were correct, but in some cases where linkage occurred, the law of independent assortment wasn't true.

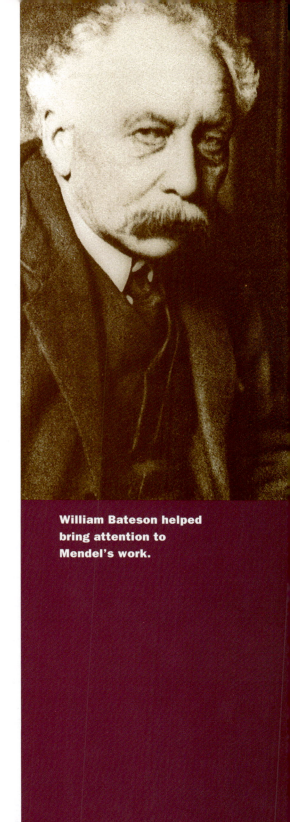

William Bateson helped bring attention to Mendel's work.

In the meantime, Mendel's champion, William Bateson, kept repeating Mendel's pea experiments to see if the laws of inheritance truly applied to the passage of traits from generation to generation. On August

Royal Families and Genetic Disorders

Royal families, in particular, have been affected by genetic disorders, or health problems that are passed down from one generation to another. One condition that plagued the British and Russian royal families was a disease called hemophilia. This disorder prevents the blood from clotting properly. While males suffer from the effects of hemophilia, the gene responsible for the illness is carried by women and is passed on to successive generations. Many relatives of England's Queen Victoria suffered from this disorder. The queen passed the gene to one son and two daughters. The daughters then passed the gene to four females, who became carriers, and to nine males, who became hemophiliacs.

The Russian and Spanish royal families were also affected by hemophilia when Queen Victoria's descendants married into these families. People who suffered the ill effects of hemophilia or carried the gene had no idea how this disease was transferred from one family member to another. In the early 1800s, the science of heredity was in its infancy. It would take Gregor Mendel and other scientists many hours of study and experimentation to discover how certain defective genes and illnesses are passed on from parent to offspring.

19, 1904, William Bateson gave an important speech at a meeting of the British Association for the Advancement of Science. He was once again defending Mendel's laws of inheritance. Bateson often said that soon every science that dealt with heredity will be teeming with discoveries that were made possible by Mendel's work.

In 1905, Bateson was asked to prepare a plan for a new school at Cambridge University for the study of heredity. This new field of science needed a name, so he invented the word "genetics," which comes from the Greek word *genetikos*, meaning "origin" or "fertile." Unfortunately, the school was never developed, but the word "genetics" became part of scientific vocabulary.

Four years after Bateson had coined the word "genetics," Wilhelm Johannsen, a professor of plant physiology at Copenhagen Agricultural College in Denmark, came up with a word of his own, "gene." People thought he had taken the word from Bateson's word, but Johannsen claimed the word was developed from Darwin's theory of pangenesis and from De Vries's word "pangen." He had just taken the last three letters of pangen and added an "e" to create the word "gene," which is the basic unit of inheritance that determines a certain trait.

William Bateson introduced other scientific words such as "zygote" to describe the fertilized egg, "homozygote" meaning "the same" (having two identical genes for a certain trait) and "heterozygote" meaning "different" (having two different genes for the same trait). He also developed a clear way to distinguish the first, second, and third hybrid generations: P1 for the parents, P2 for their offspring, and P3 for P2's offspring.

This statue is one of the many tributes to Mendel for his contributions to science.

In the summer of 1906, Bateson gave a speech at the Third International Conference on Hybridization and Plant Breeding. He presented his views on the creation of a new school of science called genetics. He stressed the importance of studying inheritance in general, along with the important work Mendel had done with his pea plants. He urged the scientific community to broaden its approach to scientific experimentation by focusing not just on plant breeding and hybridization, but on genetics as well. Scientists agreed with Bateson.

In 1908, Bateson was offered the position of professor in Cambridge's new department of genetics. He taught for two years, and then accepted a better paying position as director of the John Innes Horticultural Institute in the town of Merton Park in southwest London. He was forty-seven years old and had been involved in the field of genetics for many years. He had grown tired of research work and was looking for something new to do. But his devotion to Gregor Mendel did not change. In 1910, he traveled to the St. Thomas Monastery in Brünn to speak at the unveiling of a Mendel memorial statue with an inscription that read "To the Investigator P. Gregor Mendel, 1822–1884, Erected in 1910 by the Friends of Science."

Although Bateson was happy to see that scientists were joining together to recognize and honor Mendel's work, there were still doubters. One of them was a British mathematician and biologist named Sir Ronald Fisher.

In 1911, when Fisher was a student at Cambridge University in England he began to voice concerns that Mendel's statistics were wrong.

He thought it might be luck or even ignorance that led Mendel to his results. At that time, Fisher's criticisms were not taken seriously, but many years later, after he had graduated from college and began to study Mendel's experiments and results seriously, he wrote a paper called "Has Mendel's Work Been Rediscovered?" Fisher believed that Mendel's ratio of three to one was just too good to be true. Fisher suggested that Mendel had altered his data to fit his theory. This announcement caused a stir in the scientific community. Some scientists supported Fisher's claims, but others who had studied Mendel's work believed that Mendel had not falsified his data. Mendel had proved that his experiments on the seven traits of peas resulted in phenotypes that were close to the ratio of three to one. For example, in experiment one on seed shape, Mendel obtained 253 hybrids from 7,324 seeds. When he counted them, Mendel found 5,474 were smooth and 1,850 were wrinkled. This gave a ratio of 2.96:1. In experiment two on seed color, out of 258 plants that gave

A New Science

Although there were some changes made to Mendel's laws of inheritance, scientists around the world agreed that Mendel's groundbreaking work with the ordinary garden pea was the foundation of a new science called genetics. Gregor Mendel had led the way. Now it was up to other dedicated scientists to open up and read the book of life.

8,023 seeds, 6,022 were yellow and 2,001 green. The ratio was 3.01:1. Mendel came up with similar averages for all of the pea traits, which produced first-generation hybrids in averages that were close to the three to one ratio. Fisher never withdrew his charges, but he did acknowledge that Mendel's contribution was a great advance in the history of biology.

EIGHT

Mendel's Legacy

If Gregor Mendel were alive today, what would he think about the advances and discoveries in the field of genetics that have been made since his death. Could he have envisioned that his work with the ordinary garden pea would lead the way to these amazing discoveries? In the 1800s and into the early 1900s the field of inheritance was in its beginning stages. Mendel did not know about chromosomes or DNA or that the elements of heredity he was studying would one day be called genes. There wasn't even a name for the study of heredity.

Gregor Mendel left behind a legacy of rigorous scientific exploration and information-gathering for others to emulate. In 1944, a group of scientists at the Rockefeller Institute in New York, led by Oswald

Mendel helped lay the foundation for the study of genetics by future scientists, such as Alfred Hershey. Hershey's work showed that DNA carried the genetic code.

Avery, conducted studies that suggested DNA was responsible for passing on genetic information from generation to generation. DNA is the chemical substance that carries the genetic code for all living things and is found in the nucleus of every living cell. But it wasn't until the early 1950s that two scientists named Alfred Hershey and Martha Chase performed experiments that clearly showed that DNA was responsible for carrying the genetic code.

Trofim Lysenko and Mendelism

In 1948, the Communist Party was the dominant political force in Czechoslovakia. Trofim Lysenko, a fifty-one-year-old Russian scientist and the Soviet Union's agricultural minister, didn't believe in Mendel's theories of inheritance and denounced Mendelism as a false science. He believed that animal, plant, and human traits were acquired through environmental influence. Lysenko's ideas were supported by the Soviet dictator, Joseph Stalin. The Communist Party dismissed Mendel's laws and tried to erase any recognition of Mendel's achievements. The monastery's greenhouse was destroyed, and the Mendel Museum, also known as the Mendelianum, in the monastery was closed. Luckily, most of Mendel's papers that survived Anselm Rambousek's flame were saved by fellow scientists. Mendel's statue was also removed from the town's square. Two years later, it was placed in a corner of the Brünn (now Brno) monastery's back courtyard. The statue remains there, overlooking the gardens where Mendel once grew his pea plants.

ADVANCE IN GENETICS

In 1953, genetics took a great leap forward when an American biologist named James Watson and a British physicist named Francis Crick determined the structure of DNA. Watson and Crick discovered that DNA had its own genetic language, which is composed of only four bases, adenine, thymine, cytosine, and guanine. These bases are the chemical

The work of James Watson (shown here with a model of DNA) and Francis Crick further advanced scientific understanding of DNA and genetic code.

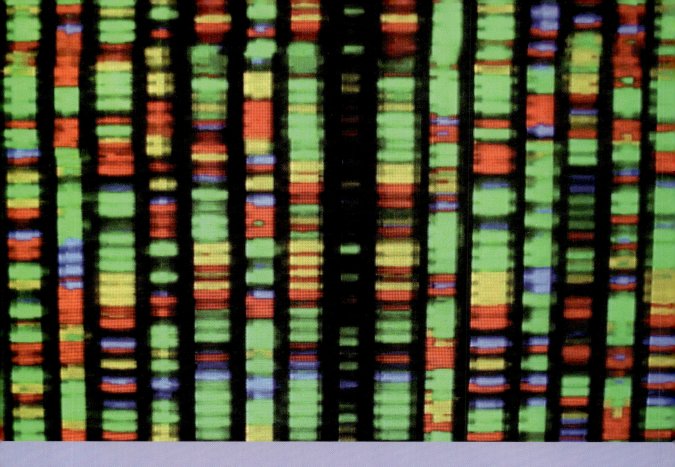

The Human Genome

Mapping the human genome means figuring out which chromosome each gene lies on and where each gene sits on that chromosome. Humans have forty-six chromosomes, twenty-three from each parent. There can be thousands of genes on each chromosome. More than three billion bases are arranged in a chemical blueprint that is determined by the order of just four letters. Each person's genome is unique and determined by the number and pattern of the bases that make up the DNA helix, or spiral. The picture above is a digital representation of the human genome.

units that are strung together to form DNA. These four chemicals are then arranged in specific order. A single mistake in the arrangement can cause a genetic disorder.

The discovery of DNA's structure opened the doors to the mapping out of human genome, or collection of genes. This occurred in 2000. Two scientists, Francis Collins and Craig Venter, announced they had mapped more than three billion letters in human DNA.

MENDEL, AN IMPORTANT SCIENTIST

Mendel probably didn't realize that he was adding the first pages to the gigantic book of life when he became interested in finding out how traits are passed from generation to generation. As he walked among his pea plants in the monastery garden, he was probably unaware of what his experiments would mean to the world and whether they would be remembered at all. Yet his laws of inheritance have influenced scientific advancements in the areas of gene therapy, screening, and testing. Gene therapy can be helpful in the diagnosis, prevention, and treatment of some genetic conditions, and genetic testing can offer people the opportunity to determine whether they carry a defective gene that they might pass on if they had children.

The Mendelianum Museum in Brno honors Mendel's memory. At the entrance to the museum is an inscription that reads "My time will come." The exhibits at the museum display books, photographs, awards, manuscripts, and notebooks relating to Mendel's life. Another more

At the museum, visitors can see some of Mendel's research materials, including Mendel's microscope.

ambitious effort to honor Gregor Mendel is taking place. There are efforts to turn part of the old Augustinian monastery into a center where scientists and researchers can meet to hold scientific conferences. There are even plans to rebuild the greenhouse that has fallen into ruin. It may take many years to achieve this goal, but dedicated scientists are working hard to make it happen.

Mendel's hometown of Hyncice has also remembered its famous inhabitant. His family home is now a state museum that features Mendel's family tree, awards, and pictures. Nearby is the village fire station, which once received a donation of 3,000 guilders from Mendel. A plaque honoring his memory was placed over the doorway in 1902.

In the United States, Mendel has also been recognized for his achievements. Villanova University in Pennsylvania has created Mendel Hall, a large center for study and research. A bronze replica of the Gregor Johann Mendel Monument in Brno sits in front of the entrance to the Mendel Science Center. The university has also established the Mendel Medal Award to recognize the scientific accomplishments of other outstanding scientists and honor Mendel's own achievements and memory. The medal was first awarded in 1929 and was presented each year until 1943. Then, until 1993, it was awarded about every two and a half years. Today, it is once again awarded annually.

In 2000, Dr. Peter C. Doherty, the 1996 Nobel Prize winner in medicine, was awarded the Mendel Medal. In 2001, Michael E. DeBakey, a world-renowned heart surgeon who has done pioneering work in artificial hearts, heart pumps, and heart transplants, was presented with the medal. In 2002, Dr. Ruth Patrick, a scientist who has done considerable research in the environmental sciences and the study

Mendel Museum of Genetics

Under the communist government, the Augustinian monks were evicted from the St. Thomas Monastery because religious communities were not allowed in Czechoslovakia. The monastery was turned into a factory, and the greenhouses and the Mendel Museum were destroyed. Furniture and books were stolen, ruined, or lost.

After the communists lost control, the Mendel Museum was reestablished in the 1960s. A collection of papers and other material that had been saved were gathered and offered in an exhibit. In the mid-1990s, a new abbot name Lukas Evzen Martinec was assigned to the monastery in what is now called the Czech Republic. Abbot Martinec realized there was a growing interest in genetics and Mendel's contributions to it. He wanted to exhibit Mendel's work in a more modern way. The Mendel exhibit has grown through the help of many people from around the world. Some of the displays included in the exhibit are a reconstructed garden showing the experiements of Mendel, William Bateson, and Hugo de Vries. Also included are meteorology instruments and Mendel's weather records and reports. In his lifetime, Gregor Mendel's science experiments did not receive the respect and recognition he is receiving in the twenty-first century.

of pollution and its effects on ecosystems, was awarded the Mendel Medal.

One of the most interesting ways in which Gregor Mendel is being remembered is at the Hospital for Sick Children in Toronto, Canada. A $4.2 million supercomputer named The Mendel is capable of helping scientists find information about the diseases that affect children. It is the largest computer in the world and can do the work of one thousand personal computers. Before The Mendel was given to the hospital through an anonymous donation, it took scientists and other computers months to find the answers to certain questions. The Mendel computer can store and analyze large amounts of information from international sources. As new data comes in, it is stored in The Mendel's memory. With the help of the computer, scientists at the hospital have identified twelve genes that play a role in diseases.

The science of genetics has taken giant leaps since those first questions asked by Gregor Mendel nearly 150 years ago. How could he know that his solitary work with the pea plants he called his "children" would help scientists and researchers uncover close to ten thousand known single-gene disorders?

Fortunately, Gregor Mendel has been remembered and honored for his experimental work on peas and the development of the basic laws of inheritance. He will always be known as the "father of genetics."

Timeline

1866 Mendel gives another speech at the Natural Sciences Society of Brünn. His paper is printed in the society's journal. He begins experimental work on the hawkweed plant.

1868 Abbot Napp dies. Mendel is elected to be the new abbot.

1870 A tornado hits the city of Brünn. Mendel writes a research paper called "The Whirlwind of Oct. 13, 1870."

1873 Europe experiences an economic crisis.

1874 Abbot Mendel becomes politically involved in a fight with the government about a new property tax levied on monasteries.

1884 Abbot Mendel dies at the age of sixty-one.

1879 Thomas Alva Edison invents the electric light.

1900 Mendel's paper on peas is rediscovered independently by three scientists.

1902 William Bateson defends the Mendelian laws of heredity. He has Mendel's paper translated into English and publishes it.

1905 Bateson plans a new school of science at Cambridge University for the study of heredity.

To Find Out More

BOOKS

Corcos, Alain F. and Floyd V. Monaghan. *Gregor Mendel's Experiments on Plant Hybrids*. Brunswick, New Jersey: Rutgers University Press, 1993.

Edelson, Edward. *Gregor Mendel and the Roots of Genetics*. New York: Oxford University Press, 1999.

Klare, Roger. *Gregor Mendel: Father of Genetics*. Springfield, New Jersey: Enslow Publishers, 1999.

Otfinoski, Steve. *The Czech Republic*. New York: Facts on File, Inc., 1997.

ORGANIZATIONS AND ONLINE SITES

Gregor Mendel Glossary
http://www.netspace.org/Mendel/web/mwgloss.html

This site offers a guide to Mendel's work, his 1865 research paper, and a genetics vocabulary.

Mendel Exhibit
http://www.library.villanova.edu/services/exhibits/mendelmedal.htm

This site provides information on Villanova University's Mendel Medal and other Mendel links.

Mendel Web
http://www.mendelweb.org

This site offers a tremendous amount of information about Gregor Mendel.

National Human Genome Research Institute
http://www.nhgri.nih.gov

This institute provides information on genetics and the mapping of the human genome.

A Note On Sources

I have researched the life and work of Gregor Mendel by doing library research, reading biographical, biology, genetics, physics, and other science books and by exploring Internet sites on Gregor Mendel and his pea experiments. Viewing a videotape on genetics was valuable in helping me understanding the human genome project. Newspaper and scientific magazine articles also contributed to the writing of this book. Mendel's paper "Experiments on Plant Hybrids" was particularly useful, as was *Gregor Mendel: The First Geneticist*, a biography written by Vitezslav Orel, emeritus head of the Mendelianum in Brno, Czech Republic. *Impact of the Gene* by Colin Tudge and *The Monk in the Garden* by Robin Marantz Henig offered further valuable information.

—*Della Yannuzzi*

Index

About the Author

Della Yannuzzi lives in Oakton, Virginia, with her husband, Michael, and their cat, J.D. She has been writing for more than thirty years. She is also a graduate of Kean College with a degree in early childhood education.

Ms. Yannuzzi has written many magazine stories. They have been published in *Highlights for Children*, *Cobblestone*, *New Moon*, *My Friend*, and others. *Gregor Mendel* is her seventh book. She enjoys writing books about people who have struggled to achieve their goals. Some of her other books are *Mae Jemison: A Space Biography*, *Zora Neale Hurston: Southern Storyteller*, *Madam C. J. Walker: Self-Made Businesswoman*, *Ernest Hemingway: Writer and Adventurer*, and *Aldo Leopold: Protector of the wild*.